T5-CVH-123

Sharks

Learning the SH Sound

Ira Wood

Phonics
for the
REAL World™

Rosen Classroom Books & Materials™
New York

A shark is a fish.

A shark has sharp teeth.

A shark eats other fish.

Sharks have many shapes.

A shark can be short.

A shark can be long.

13

Sharks live in the ocean.

You may see a shark from a ship.

You may see a shark at the zoo.

Can you see the shark?

Word List

shapes
shark
sharp
ship
short

Instructional Guide

Note to Instructors:
One of the essential skills that enable a young child to read is the ability to associate letter-sound symbols and blend these sounds to form words. Phonics instruction can teach children a system that will help them decode unfamiliar words and, in turn, enhance their word-recognition skills. We offer a phonics-based series of books that are easy to read and understand. Each book pairs words and pictures that reinforce specific phonetic sounds in a logical sequence. Topics are based on curriculum goals appropriate for early readers in the areas of science, social studies, and health.

Letter/Sound: sh – Write and pronounce **sh**. Ask the child what the sound means. Have them listen to the following words and put their finger to their lips when they hear the **sh** sound: *silly, shelf, shame, chicken, ship, shoot, shell, same, shoe, shack, shade, chop,* etc. As the child responds, list **sh** words on a chalkboard or dry-erase board.

Phonics Activities: Have the child tell whether they hear **sh** at the beginning or the end of the following words: *fish, shop, push, she, shovel, dish, shell, wish, rush, cash,* etc. As the child responds, list words in two columns according to the location of **sh**. Have the child underline **sh** in each word.
- Have the child name the long vowel sound or short vowel sound they hear in the following initial **sh** words: *shine, shape, shop, sheep, she, sheet, shake, shot, ship, shut, show,* etc. Write words in lists according to their vowel sounds. Have the child name and underline the vowel in each word.
- Present flash cards of several one-syllable words: *same, more, me, line, jeep, tip, well, mop, dock, back,* etc. Have the child name **sh** words that rhyme with the flash-card words. Write each response beside its rhyming word. Cut the flash cards in two to make a set of rhyming word puzzles as an independent activity.

Additional Resources:
- DK Publishing Staff. *Shark Attack!* New York: DK Publishing, Inc., 1998.
- Fowler, Allan. *The Best Way to See a Shark.* Danbury, CT: Children's Press, 1995.
- Prevost, John F. *Great White Sharks.* Minneapolis, MN: ABDO Publishing Company, 1995.
- Prevost, John F. *Whale Sharks.* Minneapolis, MN: ABDO Publishing Company, 1995.

Published in 2002 by The Rosen Publishing Group, Inc.
29 East 21st Street, New York, NY 10010

Copyright © 2002 by The Rosen Publishing Group, Inc.

All rights reserved. No part of this book may be reproduced in any form without permission in writing from the publisher, except by a reviewer.

Book Design: Ron A. Churley

Photo Credits: Cover, pp. 9 (center and lower), 19 © SuperStock; pp. 3, 17 © David Fleetham/FPG International; pp. 5, 15 © Image Bank; p. 7 © David Fleetham/Index Stock; p. 9 (upper) © Telegraph Colour Library/FPG International; pp. 11, 13 © James Watt/Animals Animals; p. 21 © R. Cummings/Index Stock.

Library of Congress Cataloging-in-Publication Data

Wood, Ira.
  Sharks : learning the SH sound / Ira Wood.
    p. cm. — (Power phonics/phonics for the real world)
  ISBN 0-8239-5921-X (lib. bdg.)
  ISBN 0-8239-8266-1 (pbk.)
  6 pack ISBN 0-8239-9234-9
  1. Sharks—Juvenile literature. 2. English language—Consonants—Juvenile literature. [1. Sharks.] I. Title. II. Series.
  QL638.9 .W65 2001
  597.3—dc21
                                    2001000191

Manufactured in the United States of America